PARTICIPANT'S GUIDE

STASI ELDREDGE

THOMAS NELSON
Since 1798

NASHVILLE   DALLAS   MEXICO CITY   RIO DE JANEIRO

Published in Nashville, Tennessee, by Thomas Nelson, Inc.

Published in association with Yates & Yates, LLP, Attorneys and Counselors, Orange, California.

ISBN-13: 978-1-4185-2754-9

Printed in the United States of America.
16 17 RRD 25 24 23 22

Contents

Introduction

I have always wanted to read a novel or enjoy a movie where the heroine was a normal, average-looking woman with an ordinary life who was *not* a concert pianist, brain surgeon, underwear model, or superhero in her spare time. I want to read about a woman like me. A woman like *you*. And I want to learn from her.

In choosing to do this study—by yourself, or better still, with a group of women—you are getting that opportunity! You will learn from the stories of women like yourself, and women not so like you. If you are doing this in a group, covenant together to make this a place of safety and confidentiality, a place where each woman is quick to listen and slow to offer advice. (Receiving advice often feels like people trying to *fix* us . . . when all we really long for is to be understood.) But whether you are working through this in a group or alone, *take your time!* Journal through the questions. After all, this is for you.

We women share so much. We have much more in common than most of us realize. It's true. We live with the mystery of hormones. (Often, when it seems we just begin to get them figured out, they change on us.) Most of us love to shop and *all* of us love a bargain. We don't so much like our hair, and we really don't like our annual appointment. (You know the one.) We love a good story and we love certain smells, and we love to go to the bathroom in groups.

And then there's the other side to us . . . the deeper side. There are times when we wake in the middle of the night to sorrow, lone-liness, and an ache for something more that largely goes unex-plained. We stop at red lights and while we wait, the ache rises to the surface again—ignoring our efforts to shame ourselves into wanting less. We are women. We think no one really understands. We tend to believe there is something deeply wrong with us. We think that if we were better somehow, then life wouldn't be so hard, painful, lonely, fill in the blank.

But what if the ache is a gift?

What if God is calling to us through the cry of our hearts that urges us to reach for that "something more" we all long for? What if the truest thing about us is that we *are* magnificent and meant to be the heroine of the story? Really.

Let's risk taking a look at the "what if." Come, journey with me into a realm of wonder and possibility, beauty, and hope . . . into the very heart of a woman.

This participant's guide was written to be used with the book *Captivating*, and as a companion for the DVD series, *Captivating: Heart to Heart*. There are twelve chapters in the book, ten chapters in the DVD series, and ten chapters in this guide. To get the most out of the experience, I suggest that you read *Captivating* in full before beginning. Then, as you do your weekly study, reread the appropriate chapter(s) before answering the questions in the corre-sponding chapters of this participant's guide.

If you are using this guide with the DVD series, watch the cor-responding chapter *after* you have done the lesson in the guide. If you are meeting in a group, read a chapter in *Captivating* and do the corresponding chapter in this participant's guide before you gather. Then watch the DVD together, and talk about it. I know that the DVDs will serve as a catalyst for sharing and deep conversation . . . conver-sations that are *heart to heart*.

The Heart of a Woman

(*Captivating,* Chapter One)

As we begin this study together, know that it is a study of *discovery*. A journey, really. For you to discover who God meant when he meant *you*. What does it mean to be a woman? What is my calling in life? What does God value? What does He want from me? What do *I* want? And is that *okay?*

We are not carbon copies of each other. Not at all. God loves diversity and he has fashioned each one of us uniquely and well. But it is a very good thing to know that we are not alone on this journey of life; we have much more in common with each other—simply because we are women—than we don't. We share more than most of us realize.

For instance, we have a feminine heart. We have to start there, because as the Scriptures tell us, the heart is the center of it all.

Look up Proverbs 4:23 and write it below.

Think about it: God created you *as a woman.* "God created man in his own image . . . male and female he created them" (Genesis 1:27). Whatever it means to bear God's image, you do so as a woman. Female. That's how and where you bear his image. And not in your body. The Trinity does not have a body. No, you bear God's image in your heart.

Is this a new thought for you?

Your *feminine* heart has been created with the greatest of all possible dignities—as a reflection of God's own heart. You are a woman to your soul, to the very core of your being. And so the journey to discover what God meant when he created woman in his image—when he created you as his woman—that journey begins with your heart. Another way of saying this is that the journey begins with *desire.*

What are some of your favorite stories or movies? In them, who do you want to be?

The stories we love reveal much of the secret desires of our deep hearts. If you take a close look, talk with the women in your life, you'll find that we share themes in our core desires. They are not all that we want and they play out differently in our lives, but in her heart of hearts, every woman longs to be *romanced,* to play an *irreplaceable role* in a heroic adventure and to *unveil beauty.*

It is right that we do, for it is in these desires that we bear the image of our God.

In the DVD, Sue shared that she related to the horse, Pilgrim, in the movie, The Horse Whisperer. *Why?*

ROMANCED

In your own words, define the desire to be romanced.

Do you remember some of the games you played as a little girl? What were some that you really enjoyed?

Are you aware of a longing to be someone's priority? What would you like that to look like?

IRREPLACEABLE

How would you describe the desire to play an irreplaceable role in a heroic adventure?

What were your dreams for your life when you were a little girl? What did you want to be or do?

Allowing yourself to dream a little bit, think about this: If you could do or be anything you wanted now, what would it be?

Let your mind drift over that idea, imagining what your life would be like if you could follow that dream, the people who would be around you. Would you characterize that dream role as one that would be easily replaced or one that is more on the side of essential?

How would your living that life impact others? How is the life you are living now *impacting others?*

BEAUTY TO UNVEIL

Who is beautiful to you and why?

Do you want to be beautiful, inside and out? Do you think you are or could be beautiful?

Describe the desire for a beauty to unveil.

The core desires that God placed in our hearts have a great dignity to them. We don't have to diminish them or be embarrassed by them, for it is in our desires that we bear the image of God. God wants us to delight in him, to seek him. God wants to be irreplaceable in our lives. God wants to reveal his beauty to us and to receive our worship.

A LOSS OF HEART

As a young woman, I, like the women around me, got busy with the business of life. I worked hard and tried harder. I slept less, aimed higher, and failed more. At church, often I was exhorted to *do* more. Be more. Be better. Follow these seven steps, these six lifestyles, these twelve concepts. But in all of my trying, I didn't feel I was growing as a woman. I just felt *tired*. I came to the place that Nicol Sponberg describes in her song "Resurrection": my life had turned cold, without life and without passion.

I know I am not alone in this. Most of us feel that we are failing in some areas of our lives, maybe even the most important areas. And aware of our deep failings, we pour contempt on our own hearts for wanting more. Oh, we long for intimacy and for adventure; we long to be the Beauty of some great story. But the desires set deep in our hearts seem like a luxury, don't they—granted only to those women who get their act together. The message to the rest of us—whether from a driven culture or a driven church—is *try harder*.

How have you felt the message of "try harder" come to you? How has it made you feel and/or expressed itself in your life?

Do you believe the message of "try harder" is coming from God? What do you honestly *believe God thinks about you/feels about you?*

How do you handle your heart when your core desires are not being met?

In all the exhortations—"Do *this*, and then you'll be a worthy woman"—we have missed the most important thing of all. We have missed the *heart* of a woman.

And that is not a wise thing to do, for as the Scriptures tell us, the heart is central. "Above all else, guard your heart, for it is the wellspring of life" (Proverbs 4:23). Above all else. Why? Because God knows that our heart is core to who we are. It is the source of all creativity, courage, and conviction. It is the fountainhead of our faith, our hope, and of course, our love. This "wellspring of life" within us is the very essence of our existence, the center of our being. Your heart as a woman is the most important thing about you. God *loves* you—more than you yet know or believe. Your heart *matters* to him.

God did not place these longings in our hearts to torment us. Rather, they reveal the secret of who we truly are and the role that is ours to play. There is so much hope here, hope to become the woman you secretly long to be, the woman who is romanced, irreplaceable, and utterly beautiful!

7

React to that thought. What if it were true?

Created Eve / Fallen Eve

(*Captivating*, Chapters Two and Three)

The story of creation is a wondrous and beautiful thing. God creates the Heavens and the earth and everything on them and in them. And his creation is utterly, perfectly glorious! Sometimes we forget that our story, the human story, begins with glory and beauty and goodness. In Genesis 1 we read the account of God setting his own image on the earth. He creates a being like himself. He creates a son.

> The LORD God formed the man from the dust of the ground and breathed into his nostrils the breath of life, and the man became a living being. (*Gen. 2:7*)

It is nearing the end of the sixth day, the end of the Creator's great labor, as Adam steps forth, the image of God, the triumph of his work. He alone is pronounced the son of God. Nothing in creation even comes close. Picture Michelangelo's *David*. He is . . . magnificent. Truly, the masterpiece seems complete. And yet, the Master says that something is not good, not right. Something is missing . . . and that something is Eve.

> And the Lord God cast a deep slumber on the human, and he slept, and He took one of his ribs and closed over the

flesh where it had been, and the Lord God built the rib He had taken from the human into a woman and He brought her to the human. (Gen. 2:21–23 *Alter*)

She is the crescendo, the final, astonishing work of God. Woman. In one last flourish creation comes to a finish not with Adam, but with *Eve*. She is the Master's finishing touch. Eve is . . . breathtaking.

Woman wasn't created as an afterthought but as the pinnacle of creation.

Before reading this, did you think that because God created woman second to man that women are second to men in the heart of God?

What does your heart do with being called the "crown of creation"?

The essence of woman is Beauty. What are some aspects of the power of Beauty that have struck you?

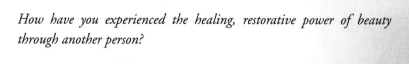

How have you experienced the healing, restorative power of beauty through another person?

Much too soon into our first parents' lives, Adam and Eve fell. They chose to disobey God and to distrust his heart.

Why did Eve take and eat the forbidden fruit, really?

Look up Genesis 3:10. Write it below.

Why was Adam afraid? What did it cause him to do?

If we understand Genesis 3:10, we understand the human condition. Every person breathing is to some extent afraid and hiding.

For women, this deep distrust of God plays out in our lives in various ways. Depending upon the story of her life, each woman tends to express her "fallenness" on a spectrum varying between being extremely controlling or extremely desolate.

We are in this together, gals. We need to look at our fallenness in order to find the redemption available to us in Christ and become the women we are intended to be. There is mercy for us. Even here.

Which way did your mother or the women who influenced you most while you were growing tend to fall? Give some examples.

Which way do you tend to go? Controlling and driven or desolate and needy?

How does that play out in your life?

The core desires that God placed in our hearts as women go largely unmet on this side of Eden. We ache. God longs for us to bring our aching hearts to him so that he can speak to and touch our deep hearts. Where do you take the ache in your heart when you don't take it to God?

Underneath our sin is a deep fear. What are you most afraid of?

Read Hebrews 4:14–16.

God knows why we do the things we do. He understands us. Look to him now with your confession. There is mercy in his eyes. He would like not only to forgive us our fallen ways, but heal our fear, and reveal his love to us in the depths of our soul where we have yet to trust him.

Wounded

(Captivating, Chapter Four)

Fallen Eve is not the truest thing about you, but we have to look at our fallenness first because it is *in the way*. It is in the way of God's desires for our lives—and our own desires—but it is not the deepest thing about us. Underneath every striving, controlling, indulging, hiding, or desolate woman is a wounded little girl.

It's true that some women's lives look perfect to us from a distance. But only from a distance. Often we are tempted to compare ourselves with other women. We compare ourselves to their looks, their lives. We can diminish the sorrow of our own personal histories by knowing a friend with a much more painful history. That is an unwise thing to do. Your life matters. Your joys, your sorrows matter.

What does Psalm 56:8 tell you about how precious your tears are to God?

Read Ecclesiastes 12:1. What does the author (Solomon) assume about "the days of trouble"?

> *"If we could read the secret history of our enemies, we should find in each man's life sorrow and suffering enough to disarm all hostility."*
>
> –HENRY WADSWORTH LONGFELLOW

We don't revisit the wounds of our lives simply to feel sorry for ourselves, but for the purposes of God to heal us. He invites us to grieve our wounds and to receive his comfort and then his healing. But to be healed, we must once again let God tenderly open our wounds and expose them to his light, to his love, and to his truth.

What are the core questions in every little girl's heart?

How was your heart handled as a little girl?

Think back through the story of your life. Can you remember an instance where you were hurt? What happened?

What did you come to believe about yourself through this event?

Was this a one-time event or did similar things happen throughout your life that reinforced the message against your heart? What were some of those events, situations or words?

The wounds that we received as young girls did not come alone. The wounds brought messages with them, messages of who you are as a woman or messages of who you will *never* be. And because they were delivered with such pain, we believed them. As children, we didn't have the faculties to process and sort through what was happening to us. If we were overwhelmed or belittled or hurt or abused, we believed that somehow it was because of *us*—the problem was with us.

Do you know what horrid things you have been wounded into believing about yourself? Try to put it/them into a sentence.

How were your heart's questions, "Am I lovely?" and "Do You delight in me?" answered in your youth?

Ask God to reveal to you the ways that believing these things has shaped your life. Has it shaped your style of relating to others? Birthed fear? Mistrust? Journal your thoughts below.

Are you ready and willing to consider that the secret, awful things you have come to deeply believe about yourself are not true *and that you did not deserve the wounds you received? Take a risk. Consider it. What if they are lies? What would that mean about you and your life?*

What if the message delivered with your wounds simply isn't true about you? Let that sink in. **It wasn't true.** What does it free you to do? Weep? Rejoice? Let go? Take your heart back?

And sisters, you still have a Question. You still want to know. *Do you see me? Am I captivating? Do I have a beauty all my own?* You must ask God what he sees. Take this to him.

Read Isaiah 62:1–5, and put your name in where the text reads "Zion" and "you." Jesus came to *heal* the brokenhearted and to set the captives free. He came for *us!* And we don't wait for all of it until we are in Heaven. Yes, then it will be perfect. No more pain. No more sorrow. No more tears. But there is *much* available for us here, now, on this side. So much.

There is hope. There is healing. There is *life*. For you. For me. For all of us. Let's turn to God now and receive the *more* that he has for us.

Healing the Wound

(Captivating, Chapter Six)

When Jesus first entered the synagogue to begin his earthly mission, he opened the Holy Scriptures and read from the book of Isaiah. When he finished, he proclaimed that in that moment, the Scripture had been fulfilled. Jesus read Isaiah 61.

Read it now for yourself: Isaiah 61, verses 1–3.

Jesus could have chosen so many Scriptures to announce his ministry and his mission yet he chose this one. Why? Because it is *central* to God's purposes and God's heart.

In your own words, what is Jesus offering?

Who is he offering it to?

When you first became a Christian, what did you think Christianity was primarily about? Did you know it is primarily about your restoration?

The offer from our God is to heal our broken hearts and to set free the places that are held captive within us. All of us have broken hearts. All of us are held captive to varying degrees. In order to receive the healing that God has for us, we must bring him our wounded hearts. ˙

Revelation 3:20 says what?

Although we primarily understand that verse in terms of our initial salvation, there are doors within our hearts that remain closed. And Jesus will come knocking. You see, Jesus is kind and gentle. Yes, he made our hearts, but he will not force healing upon us. There are chambers in our heart that remain locked from the inside, and Jesus waits for us to invite him in *there*, to give him access.

Are you willing and ready to give him deeper access to your heart in order to heal you? What would you like to invite Jesus into, to heal you? Write it below, be specific.

Jesus heals our hearts through many ways and through many people. Receiving counseling from a caring believer has been helpful for many Christians. The Holy Spirit is called the Counselor and will come to us through the Word of God and in the quiet places of our hearts. Other people find healing and courage in a God-given strength to attempt something challenging. In the DVD, Sue shares that God was doing a work of healing in her heart through ballroom dance classes. It took enormous courage for her to begin, but God has met her every step of the way. Dream a little of what that might look like for you.

How might God be inviting your heart to come alive?

The thoughts we entertain and give ascent to are incredibly important. They shape our faith, our relationships, and our very lives.

What does 2 Corinthians 10:5 instruct us to do?

God wants us, commands us rather, to take every thought captive before him, to make all in *agreement with him*. It is his Word and his judgment on our deep hearts that alone is true.

What does Romans 8:1 say? Do you choose now to believe it?

What lies have you been believing that you must renounce making agreements with? Write them here, then pray, breaking those agreements.

Some of us need to allow ourselves to cry. Augustine, in his *Confessions,* wrote: "The tears streamed down and I let them flow as freely as they would, making for them a pillow for my heart." There was a time in my life when I was afraid to grieve, afraid to feel the pain I had buried in my heart for fear that once I began to cry, I would be unable to stop. It wasn't true. Let your tears come. Give yourself some time.

For some of us, our not being able to truly forgive those that hurt us remains in the way of our healing. We know that Jesus commands us to forgive, but still it is so hard. We need to understand that by forgiving those who wounded us, we are not saying it didn't matter. No. It mattered. Deeply. But as long as we refuse to forgive, we remain their prisoner and they continue to hurt us.

Look up Colossians 3:13. What does it say?

Jesus' blood cleanses us from all our sin. It covers all wrongs we have committed. It cleanses us from all acts we have done or should have done but didn't. It is also enough to cleanse us from the sins of others.

Let's pray.

My dear Jesus, thank you for forgiving me all my sins at the cross. Please help me to forgive others as well. It's hard, Lord. But you do it. Would you please forgive them through me? Jesus, by your grace, with your strength and in your Name, I forgive _____ for _____. I release them to you. I lay them down at your feet. I bring your cross and your blood between us. Please cleanse me of my sin again, and cleanse me of theirs. Forever. In Jesus' name, I pray. Amen.

Now, for the best part. We've given Jesus access to our broken hearts, we've invited him in, we've renounced the agreements we have made with the lies planted in our souls (even if they still feel true). So now, we ask Jesus to heal us

Go ahead. Ask him.

Then, ask him to answer your questions: How do you see me? Am I a captivating woman? Now, wait for His answer.

You will be a crown of splendor in the LORD's hand,
a royal diadem in the hand of your God.
No longer will they call you Deserted,
or name your land Desolate.
But you will be called Hephzibah (my delight is in her!)
and your land Beulah (married);
for the LORD will take delight in you,
and your land will be married.

Isaiah 62:3–4, with commentary

Spiritual Warfare

(Captivating, Chapters Four and Eleven)

If you will listen carefully to any woman's story, you will hear a theme: The assault on her heart. It might be obvious, as in the stories of physical, verbal, or sexual abuse. Or it might be more subtle, the indifference of a world that cares nothing for her, but *uses* her until she is drained. Forty years of neglect damages a woman's heart, too, dear friends. Either way, the wounds continue to come long after we've "grown up," but they all seem to speak the same message. Our Question is answered again and again throughout our life, the message driven home into our hearts like a stake.

What is to account for the systemic, often brutal, nearly universal assault on femininity? Where does this *come* from? Do not make the mistake of believing that "men are the enemy." Certainly men have had a hand in this, and will have a day of reckoning before their Maker. But you will not understand this story—or *your* story—until you begin to see the actual Forces behind this, and get a grip on their motives.

Where do you think the hatred for women you see all over the world comes from? Why is it so diabolical?

Read 1 Peter 5:8. What is Peter assuming is happening to our brothers and sisters around the world?

Spiritual warfare is no strange thing. It is not reserved for the few, the leaders of the world and the church. It is a normal part of the Christian life. For every Christian. Paul assumes that every Christian is under regular, spiritual assault. It is a normal part of the Christian life. It's true. And it's true for you.

Look up John 10:10. Write the whole verse below.

Too often, in church, we only hear about the second part of this verse. But Jesus said them in the same breath. In order to have the life that Jesus wants for us to have, we have to be aware that we have an enemy who is busy about trying to steal, kill, and destroy our lives and the lives of those we know and love.

What are the two factors we've already discussed that suggest Satan has a special hatred for women?

How have you felt spiritually attacked as you've done this study or gathered with your women's group? Common accusations from the enemy could be "You are talking too much," "You are not talking enough," "You aren't spiritual enough," "They don't like you," and "You don't fit in here." Sound familiar?

James 4:7 says to do what? What is a prerequisite to having the devil flee?

Read Ephesians 6:10–18. Why would Paul tell us to put on the full armor of God?

There is a struggle. There is a battle. And you are in it. In fact, the story of your life, of every woman's life, is the story of the long and sustained assault upon her heart by the one who knows who she could be and fears her. You are under regular, spiritual assault. When you believe that the devil has no fiery darts flying your way, then you believe that every wicked, hurtful thing that comes your way is either your fault or God's. You end up blaming God for things the devil is doing, and your view of the good, faithful, loving heart of God is badly skewed. It destroys your relationship with him. And the devil just loves that.

*What have you believed about God that is **not true** and has hurt your relationship with him? (Think hard—we all have something!)*

The whole point in battling spiritual warfare is not to focus on the devil but to free us to *love Jesus*. Jesus, our King, is always the point.

It is time to wake up and rise up. We desperately need to become aware of the enemy's schemes against us and all those we love. We must put on the armor of God every day. And stand firm in the truth. Resist the devil. Command him and his minions to depart—out loud—in the name of our Savior, Jesus Christ. Revelation 12:11 tells us that we overcome Satan by the blood of the Lamb and the word of our testimony.

Read Colossians 2:15. What has been done to the enemy?

Read 1 John 4:4. Who is stronger?

Read Colossians 1:13–14. What has God done for you?

Read Romans 8:15. What do you have?

Read 1 Peter 5:8. We have the victory in Jesus. But the devil still does what?

Demons are like sharks when there is blood in the water. We get hurt, we get sick, we sin, and the demons come along and try to make it worse by putting their evil spin on our circumstances. Self-accusation, self-contempt, and shame are common weapons in their arsenal of hatred. Their goal is to separate us from God, from each other, and from our true selves.

Read Ephesians 6:10. What are we instructed to be?

Try to put words to the theme *of the assault against your life.*

What in your life might be warfare that you hadn't considered before?

In order to have the life God wants for you, you must rise up and take your stand in him. There is a fierceness that God placed in women and *this* is what it is for. Men aren't our enemy. People are not the enemy. But you have one. There is no reason to fear him, but you must not close your eyes, plug your ears and hope he just goes away. He won't. *You* must **resist**.

Romanced

(Captivating, Chapter Seven)

There comes a time in the life of every believer when propositional truth is no longer enough. It will always remain central, the foundation for our faith. And sometimes it is all we have, and we can run far and long on it. But we are made for intimacy *with* God, not just knowledge *about* him. As women, we long for romance. We are wired for it; it's what makes our hearts come alive. The path of our restoration as women, the healing of our feminine hearts, takes us into a deeper experience of God and his love for us.

How comfortable are you with the idea of Jesus being your "Bridegroom" and you being his Beloved? Is this a relatively new "category" for you to think in about your relationship with him?

Read Isaiah 62:1–5, again substituting your name for "Zion." What new name does God call you?

OPENING OUR HEARTS TO THE ROMANCER

Let yourself dream a little. What would be an incredibly romantic day or evening for you?

    I imagine that whatever you described, it included intimacy and beauty. You were not alone and you were in some lovely place that takes your breath away. To have this dream come true doesn't mean you need to wait for a man.

    God is the author of romance. It is his idea and he is the best at it. It is wonderful to be in a loving relationship with a man, to share life, to have romance and intimacy in tangible ways. Our deep longing can be met . . . momentarily. But as David Wilcox sings, "There's a hole in your cup." No matter how much a man pours into our hearts, we still long for more. Whatever our marital status, the deep longing for romance and intimacy remains. Only God can meet it in the deepest and most substantive, life-changing way.

    God longs to bring this into your life himself. He wants us to move beyond "Jesus loves me, this I know, for the Bible tells me so." He wants to heal us through his love to become mature women who actually know him. Our hearts are desperate for this—to experience for ourselves that the truest thing about his heart toward us is not disappointment or disapproval but deep, fiery, passionate love. This is, after all, what a woman was made for.

What do you love? Where is your favorite place?

What is a favorite memory of yours? (Sometimes remembering a time from our childhood that was good can be difficult. Ask for God's help here if you're experiencing this.)

Where do you feel most alive?

Every song you love, every memory you cherish, every moment that has moved you to holy tears has been given to you from the One who has been pursuing you from your first breath in order to win your heart. God's version of flowers and chocolates and candlelight dinners comes in the form of sunsets and falling stars, moonlight on lakes and cricket symphonies, warm wind, swaying trees, lush gardens, and fierce devotion.

This is immensely personal. It will be—has been—tailor made to your heart. He knows what takes your breath away, knows what makes your heart beat faster. We have missed many of his notes simply because we shut our hearts down in order to endure the pain. Now, in our healing journey as women, we must open our hearts again, and keep them open. Not foolishly, not to anyone and anything. But yes, we must choose to open our hearts again so that we might hear his whispers, receive his kisses.

Read Hosea 2:14 and write it here.

What would you love for God to say tenderly to you?

Read the following verses and write below how God describes you or himself.

Ephesians 1:4–5

Song of Songs 4:1

Hosea 2:16

Song of Songs 5:1

You are the one who overwhelms his heart with just one glance of your eyes (Song of Songs 4:9). You are the one He sings over with delight and longs to dance with across mountaintops and ballroom floors (Zephaniah 3:17). You are the one who takes his breath away by your beautiful heart that against all odds hopes in Him. You are the Beloved of Jesus and he *is* your Knight in Shining Armor. Let that be true for a moment. Let is be true for you, of you.

How has your vision of Christianity changed since you first became a Christian?

How does the revelation that Christianity is primarily about an invitation from God to a life of intimacy and romance with God change things for you?

In the DVD series, Julie shared that reading the book *The Sacred Romance* by Brent Curtis and John Eldredge opened up the gospel to her in new ways. "This is something I could give my life to," she said. If you haven't read this book, I *highly* recommend it to you.

Below, flesh out what we mean by a woman's desire to be romanced. (It is so much more than candlelit dinners and heart-shaped boxes of chocolates!)

How is the Romance coming to you these days?

One of the ways that God romances us is by answering our Question. Keep asking Jesus the core questions of your heart: "Do you delight in me? Am I captivating to you?"

What would you love God to restore to you?

In order to have intimacy with Jesus, you must offer it to him. How? Cultivate an adoring heart. In Matthew 22:37, what does Jesus say is the greatest commandment? What does your God most want from you?

What is your most precious commodity? How can you offer that to God?

For most of us, our most precious commodity is our *time*. One of the best ways to cultivate an adoring heart is to set aside time each week to spend alone with Jesus. During that time, focus your heart on the attributes of God. Thank him for who he is and what he has done. Tell him why you think he is wonderful. Offer him your heart.

God is not after servants who love, but lovers who serve. What does this mean to you?

Loving a Man

(*Captivating,* Chapter Nine)

Every woman has men in her life. They may be her father, her husband, her brother, her son, her neighbor, or a coworker. Men do make up the other half of the population, you know. They are around. And I think it's safe to say that all of us have room for improvement in our relationships with men. I mean, they say women are a mystery. But are not men a mystery as well? They are *different* from us in some very core ways; not just in ways that are cultural and social, but in the ways they tend to think and view the world.

So many problems come into our relationships with men simply from not understanding one another.

Do boys and men want to be delighted in? What is the core question of every little boy and every man's heart?

In the DVD, Morgan shares about his two-year-old son Joshua and two things that he wanted from his father. What were they?

Who are the key men in your life? How was their Question answered for them in their youth?

If you do not know the story of your husband's life, it will be so hard to understand who he is and why he makes the choices he does. I encourage you to *invite* your husband to hear your story, and for you to hear his. Set apart a whole evening for this. Preferably two. Give yourselves at least two hours each. And then share your history from birth, through early childhood, school, friends, everything that God reminds you of, share. Have Kleenex nearby. And pray together before you begin.

How has that played out in their lives?

Can a woman answer the core question of a man's heart?

Fallen Eve is expressed in women on the spectrum from controlling and driven to desolate and needy. How is fallenness expressed in men? What is their "spectrum"?

What can a woman do to encourage and strengthen men?

What do men most need from women?

In the DVD, the men shared ways that they want to be loved, including being respected and trusted. The number one way they shared that a woman can love a man is by loving herself and making her relationship with Jesus her priority. What strikes you about this? What were some other ways they shared that they want to be loved?

Read Ephesians 5:1. What does living a life of love mean to you regarding your relationships with men?

How do men NOT want to be treated by women?

Can a man truly answer the core questions in a woman's heart?

Read 1 Peter 3:6. How does this verse relate to living a life of love?

Luring Adam to the heart of God can be done by women in countless ways. It can even be done without a word. Women can lead and love by the example of their lives, primarily by growing in relationship with Christ.

God wants us to encourage one another, to love each other into becoming the man or woman that he created us to be.

Beauty to Unveil

(Captivating, Chapter Eight)

Beauty is a hard subject for women to talk about. Our desire for beauty has caused us countless tears and untold pain. The world's view of beauty is unattainable for the majority of women . . . and yet we long for it.

The Bible teaches that every woman is made in the image of God. Every woman bears his image in her heart and carries within her the very essence of Beauty. Apart from God, beauty gets twisted, used and abused. Being beautiful on the outside doesn't mean a woman has a beautiful heart.

Look up 1 Samuel 16:7 and write it here.

What is of the utmost importance to God?

When we receive Jesus Christ as our Savior, through faith, we become a new creation (2 Corinthians 5:17). Our hearts are circumcised unto God (Romans 2:29), and God replaces our hearts of stone with a heart of flesh (Ezekiel 36:26). According to Ephesians 3:17, where then does Christ dwell?

Read Proverbs 27:19. What does it mean?

Is God beautiful? Base your answer on Scripture.

When we speak of strength as being the essence of masculinity, we are not talking about big muscles. In the same way, when we speak of beauty as being the essence of femininity, we are not talking about a woman's outward features.

If God dwells in your heart by faith, and God is altogether lovely, what does that say about your new heart?

OK. Take a moment and let this sink in. You have a beauty all your own. You bear God's image and you *are* beautiful. Inside. *And* out. It is true.

Do you want to be beautiful? Do you believe you are?

In the DVD, Lori shares that she is growing in owning her beauty, seeing glimpses of it. She said, "I know God loves me and if He can delight in me, then there's something there." God is delighting in you as well.

Do your friends think you are beautiful? Does God?

49

This isn't about dresses and makeup. For now, don't you recognize that a woman yearns to be *seen* and to be thought of as captivating? We desire to possess a beauty that is worth pursuing, worth fighting for, a beauty that is core to who we *truly* are. We want beauty that can be seen; beauty that can be felt; beauty that affects others; a beauty all our own to unveil.

The desire to be beautiful is an ageless longing. God has set eternity in our hearts. The longing to be beautiful is set there as well.

Who is a woman who is beautiful to you? Why?

A beautiful woman is a woman whose heart is alive.

In the DVD, Leigh shared that she first learned about Corrie Ten Boom in The Hiding Place. *Corrie Ten Boom is an amazing woman but it was her sister, Betsy, who captured Leigh. Do you remember why?*

It is a rare woman who knows and is comfortable with her beauty. Let's pray now and invite God into this place where so many of us have been so deeply wounded and continue to struggle.

Dear God,

You are beautiful and I believe I bear your image. But you know that I don't feel very pretty let alone beautiful. Would you please come to this place in my heart . . . this core place . . . and reveal to me my own beauty? Please heal the places in my heart that have been assaulted and hurt regarding beauty. And establish your truth here. Do you think I'm beautiful? How? Why? Please help me, Jesus. It's in your name that I pray.
Amen

Read 1 Peter 3:3–5. What is the "unfading beauty of a gentle and quiet spirit"?

The KEY for women to live by faith and be able to offer their inner beauty and their outer beauty to others is given to us in 1 Peter 3:6. What does Peter instruct us to not give way to?

In the depths of your heart, the secret places within, what are you afraid of?

How has fear kept you from living a life of love and offering your true beauty?

Are you ready to ask God to replace your fear with faith? Go ahead, pray.

In the DVD, Leigh says that for her to "stop hiding" would mean to believe that others need her. She would then be forced to risk offering. It's true. Others do need Leigh. And others do need *you.*

A woman in her glory, a woman of beauty, is a woman who is not striving to become beautiful or worthy or enough. She knows in her quiet center where God dwells that He finds her beautiful, has deemed her worthy and in Him, she is enough.

She exudes a sense of calm, a sense of rest, and invites those around her to rest as well. She speaks comfort, that all is well, that all will be well. *A woman of true beauty offers others the grace to be and the room to become.*

This is why we must keep asking. Ask Jesus to show you your beauty. Ask him what he thinks of you *as a woman.* His words to us let us rest. And unveil our beauty.

Irreplaceable Role

(Captivating, Chapter Twelve)

A woman doesn't come alive being merely *useful.* We want our lives to matter and to matter deeply. We want to be *needed. Irreplaceable.* And so does God.

Read Genesis 1:28. To whom did God give this command?

How important are women to the unfolding Story that God is telling?

EZER KENEGDO

In Genesis 2:18, God says that it is not good for man to be alone: "I will make a helper suitable for him." How have you understood the word "helper," and how has being created as a helper to man made you feel?

Many women have felt irritated, rebellious, even "less than" men from this verse about being created as a "helpmeet." The reason for this stems primarily from the fact that we haven't understood what God was saying. We need to restore the dignity to women in the creation story by reclaiming the glory of the word *helpmeet*.

When God creates Eve, he calls her an *ezer kenegdo*. "It is not good for the man to be alone, I shall make him a [*ezer kenegdo*]" (Genesis 2:18). Alter is getting close when he translates it "sustainer beside him."

The word *ezer* is used only twenty other places in the entire Old Testament. And in every other instance, the person being described is God himself, when you need him to come through for you *desperately*. A better translation therefore of *ezer* would be "life-saver." *Kenegdo* means alongside, or opposite to, a counterpart.

Read Psalm121:1–2, Psalm 33:20, and Psalm 115:9–11. What does the psalmist need from God?

You see, the life God calls us to is not a safe life. Why else would we need him to be our *ezer*? You don't need a life-saver if your mission is to be a couch potato. You need an *ezer* when your life is in constant danger. *Ezer* is woven into the fabric of your feminine heart. You must live this out.

How does this truer definition of "helpmeet" affect you?

Who is your favorite woman in the Bible and why?

Who are some women who are your present-day heroes? Why?

As we grow in Christ and become more and more his,

more healed and more truly ourselves, God recovers and restores our desires. And if we never have been aware of any, he awakens them. Not all women are mothers, but all women are life-givers. Women give birth to all kinds of things: ministries, relationships, creative works, books . . . the list is endless.

What would you like to give birth to?

God has written something on your heart. Giving yourself permission to dream, think: If you could do anything, what would it be? Where? Who else might be involved?

If you don't know what your calling is, what God has written on your heart, look at how you have been wounded in your life. What has been assaulted? What lies have been spoken to you? These wounds often reveal the secret of your glory and what you are meant to bring to the world. Why else would you be so attacked there?

Some of the desires that God has written on our heart are specific and some are mythic. In the DVD, Julie shares that as a little girl she wanted to be a nurse. She sees now that although she is not a nurse, she is still affecting change in people by bringing the healing of Jesus Christ that is available to people.

What did you dream of being when you were younger?

56

Are you living that out now?

Sometimes God will give us a dream or a vision for our lives, then ask us to lay it down. He is *always* after our hearts . . . bringing about our healing and our restoration. He wants to be the priority in our lives, our First Love. When he asks us to lay something down, he will often bring it back to us later . . . only refined and *better*.

How is the life you are living today affecting others for good?

In the DVD, Leigh shares the analogy about the Academy Awards, the world's most mythic night. What strikes you about this analogy and your desires for romance, a role to play and a beauty to unveil?

All women have an irreplaceable role to play and are called to be life-givers. The way we live this out expresses itself in a myriad of ways throughout our lives. You are a woman. You are a life-giver. You *do* have an irreplaceable role to play. We need you. God needs you. Choose Him. First. Last. And in between.

Caring for Your Heart

(Captivating, Chapter One)

The journey of life is a wonderful, beautiful, and often excruciatingly painful one. In the midst of all the demands and pressures that we feel, often the first thing we abandon is caring for our hearts. And that is a dangerous thing to do.

Write Proverbs 4:23 here, in your own words.

God instructs us to guard our hearts, as in to *protect* them, *shield* them, *watch over* them, *nurture* them, *care* for them. It is in our heart of hearts that all life flows. It is in our hearts that Jesus makes his home and it is from our hearts that all love, all creativity, all worthy endeavors flow. It is of the utmost importance to God and therefore, should be to us.

How can we care for our hearts?

As followers of Christ, the best way that we nourish our hearts and grow in Him is by spending *time* with Him.

In the DVD, we share what doing this study together has been like. Were you surprised by our answers? What has your experience been like doing this study?

Although we share much in common as women, we are each also uniquely fashioned. Some of the things that feed my spirit may not be a source of life to you. I need regular time outside, alone, in the beauty of creation. I love to garden. I need time away, alone with God. I love being around horses. I love bubble baths. I love to paint. Now I can't do these things every single day, but I must make room for them in my life. Otherwise, I slip into living a life of duty and obligation, and the joy, the love, the heart goes out of my life.

What do you enjoy? What feeds your spirit?

If you had the time, every single week, to do something that you love to do, what would it be?

In order to play the role that is yours to play and in order to fight for the hearts of others, you will need to care for your heart. But know in advance that all movements toward God and toward Life are opposed. You will need to pray for God's help here—and press through.

FRIENDSHIPS OF WOMEN

What does Hebrews 10:25 say to do?

Many people interpret this verse as an instruction to participate in corporate worship, but this goes way beyond *attending* a church service once a week. This means to live your life in fellowship with other believers. We cannot go it alone. We need each other. Are you in a small group? Do you have a couple of friends who really know you, know your story, know your struggles, know your glory? You need to. If you don't, pray. Ask God for them and keep your eyes open, for he will bring them.

Look up Ephesians 5:19. What does it say should occupy our thoughts, our words?

How have the friendships of women helped you?

Now, I know that friendships have been and can be a great source of joy in your life, but they can also be a great source of pain. We are, after all, human. Friendships falter. Friends can bless but they can also betray. The waters get murky when we laden our friendships with our deepest desires for connection and intimacy. We will have golden moments of connection. But only moments. They will come again . . . but we cannot demand perfection now. Perfect relationships free from misunderstanding and judgment are coming. We get to practice now. Love your friends and enjoy your friendships for what they are. Pray for them to go deeper, to increase. But don't dismiss them for not being what you most deeply long for. That my sister, *is* coming.

In the DVD we say that friendships are opposed. They must be fought for. Has this been your experience?

How can you become a better friend? Who would you like to touch most, but haven't? Which friend do you wish were closer?

Do you need or want to grow in your ability to be present? *Ask God to help you.*

LIVING TOGETHER WITH JESUS

God wants to live this life together with you, to share in your days and decisions, your desires and disappointments. He wants intimacy with you in the midst of the madness and mundane, the laundry and lists, the carpools and conversations, and projects and pain. He wants to pour his love into your heart, and he longs to have you pour yours into his. He wants your deep heart—that center place within that is the truest *you.*

We were born into a world at war. The battle is the Lord's, and he was and is and will be victorious. But it hasn't all played out. He needs you to bring his kingdom here on earth. It is a holy partnership. He won't force you to join him. But he invites you.

How is Jesus inviting you to join him? What will it require of you?

What is your answer?

Closing Remarks

Well, you've finished. Well done! I hope this journey through *Captivating* has taken you deeper into the heart of God *for you*. You will want to stay with the messages that have stirred you for a while…don't just run on to the next thing, whatever that may be. God wants to continue moving in and through your life, healing you, restoring you, wooing you, deeply and intimately. I want to encourage you to keep asking him the deep questions of your heart. Don't worry. He never gets tired of us asking. He loves the dialogue! Hold on to what God has said and done throughout this study and to what he most values—*you*, your heart. Your heart is the treasure of the kingdom. And remember that at the heart of Christianity is *romance*. When we have the eyes of our hearts opened to this beautiful reality, it changes everything, doesn't it?! You've finished the study, but today is only the beginning or rather, the continuation of an amazing, wonderful life with God. Maybe it's your turn to invite a few gals to go through this study with you! But wherever and however the Lord leads you, go with Jesus…partnering with him in bringing his Kingdom while the invitation to you always remains to go farther up and farther in. Hooray!

With you, for you and in *Him*,

Stasi

About the Author

Stasi Eldredge's heart was captured by God through the Sacred Romance and she has never gotten over it. Or rather, Him. Her books include *Becoming Myself* and *Love & War* (coauthored with her husband John). Their ministry, Ransomed Heart, has been used by God to transform the lives of men and women all over the world. They make their home in Colorado. The mother of three grown sons who no longer live in her home but take residence forever in her heart, Stasi is a writer and conference speaker passionate about women embracing the value of their heart and life to Jesus Christ and risking everything on that!